THIS BOOGER BOOK
BELONGS TO:

____

CREATED, PUBLISHED, AND DISTRIBUTED BY KNOCK KNOCK
6695 GREEN VALLEY CIRCLE, #5167
CULVER CITY, CA 90230
KNOCKKNOCKSTUFF.COM
KNOCK KNOCK IS A REGISTERED TRADEMARK OF KNOCK KNOCK LLC

PRINTED IN CHINA

TEXT AND ILLUSTRATIONS BY DAN GOLDEN

MIX
Paper | Supporting responsible forestry
FSC® C008047
FSC www.fsc.org

ISBN: 978-168349535-2
UPC: 825703503272

CC-01/2025-01

THE ONLY BOOGER BOOK YOU'LL EVER NEED

DAN GOLDEN

KNOCK KNOCK® Kids
knockknockstuff.com

TABLE OF CONTENTS

INTRODUCTION

AKA THE "BOOGERDUCTION"

HEY THERE!

WHY AM I SO OBSESSED WITH BOOGERS? IS IT THEIR OOEY-GOOEY TEXTURE? THEIR VIBRANT COLOR? THEIR UNIQUE UMAMI FLAVOR? OR IS IT JUST BECAUSE THEY'RE THESE WEIRD LITTLE BLOBS THAT LIVE IN MY NOSE?

WHATEVER THE REASON, I'M SURE YOU'D AGREE THAT BOOGERS ARE THE MOST AMAZING THINGS TO HAVE EVER EXISTED. RIGHT?

SO GET READY TO DIG INTO THE WONDERFUL WORLD OF BOOGERS! FROM BOOGER ART AND BOOGER MATH TO THE SECRET LIVES OF BOOGERS, THIS BOOK HAS IT ALL. AND THAT'S WHY IT'S THE ONLY BOOGER BOOK YOU'LL EVER NEED.

I HOPE YOU HAVE AS MUCH FUN READING IT AS I DID MAKING IT.

YOUR BOOGER FRIEND,

DAN GOLDEN
(WRITING FROM MY HOME ON BOOGER ISLAND)

HOW TO IDENTIFY A BOOGER

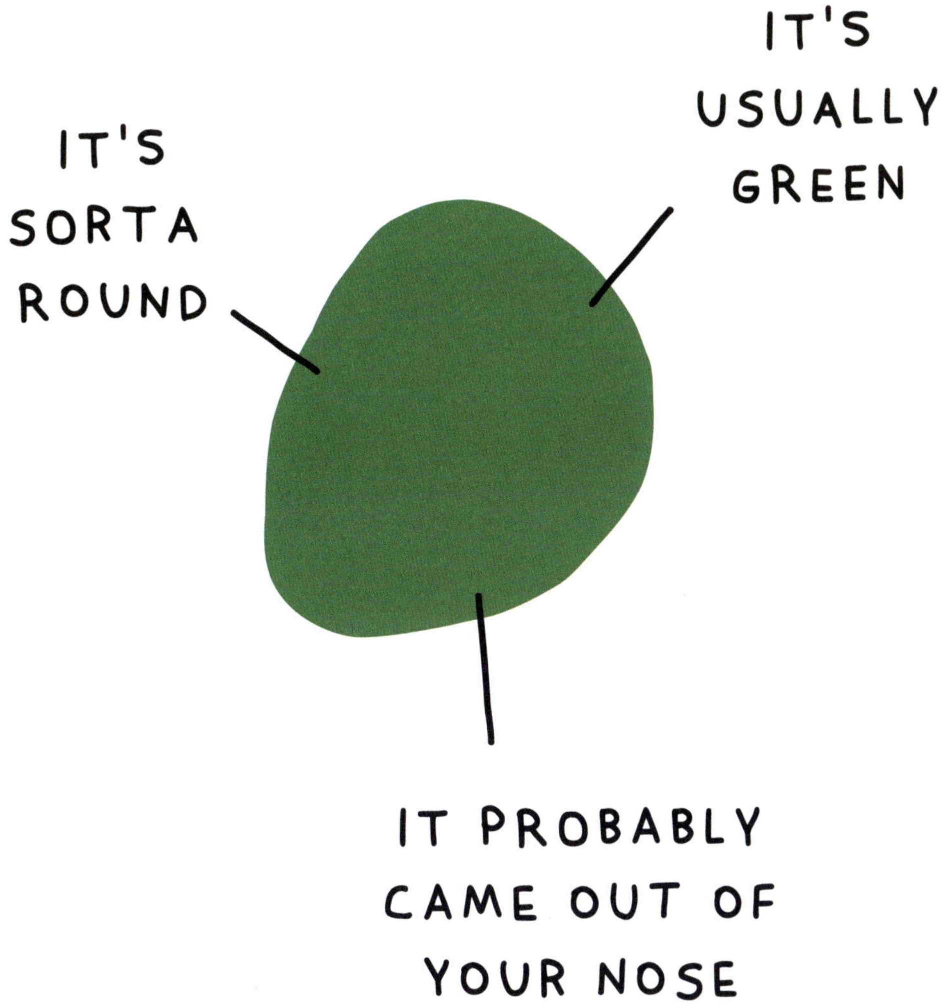
IT'S SORTA ROUND
IT'S USUALLY GREEN
IT PROBABLY CAME OUT OF YOUR NOSE

WHAT ARE BOOGERS MADE OF?

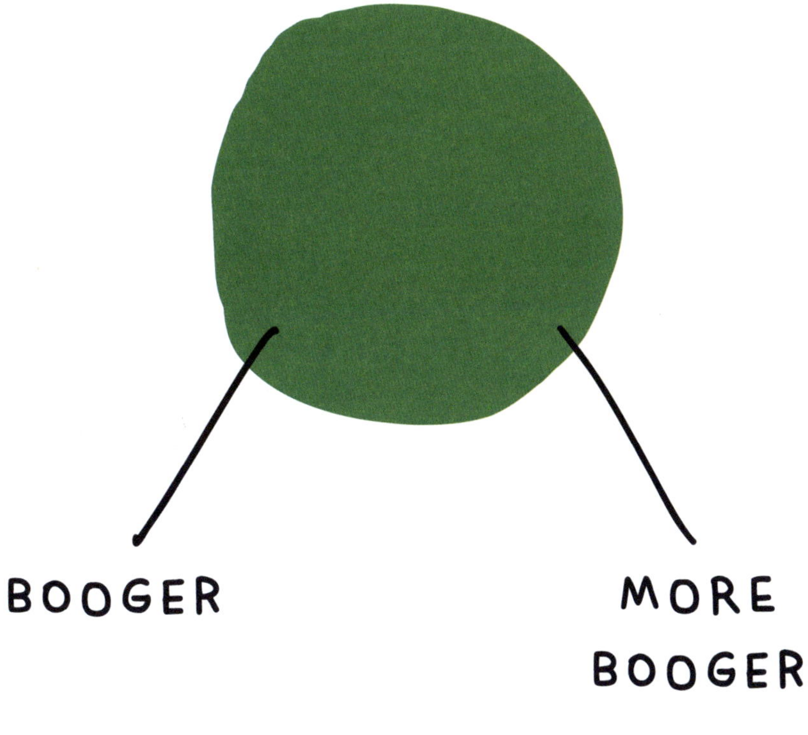
BOOGER
MORE BOOGER

BOOGERS COME
IN MANY SHADES

WHICH CAME FIRST, THE BOOGER OR THE NOSE?

BIRTH OF A BOOGER

THE TRADITIONAL BOOGER FAMILY

THE LIFE CYCLE OF A BOOGER

YOUTH

MIDDLE AGE

OLD AGE

THE PERFECT BOOGER

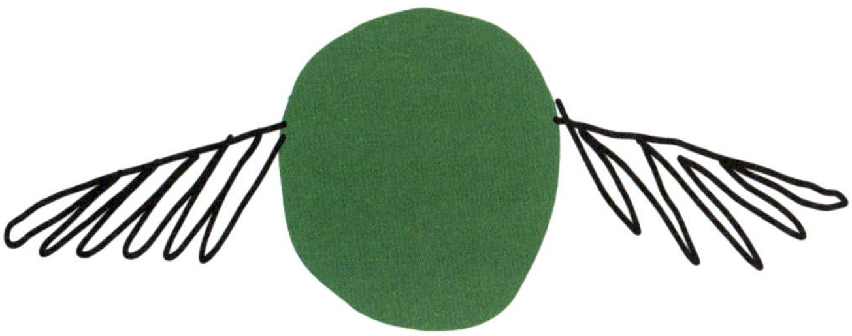

A RARE
FLYING BOOGER

A BOOGER TO WATCH OUT FOR

WHAT'S FOR BREAKFAST, MA?
BOOGER JAM AND TOAST!
YAY!

LEARNING TO COUNT WITH BOOGERS

ONE BOOGER

TWO BOOGERS

THREE BOOGERS

FOUR BOOGERS

FIVE BOOGERS

x =

SIX BOOGERS!

PROFESSOR HAROLD KESLER

ESTEEMED DOCTOR, LECTURER, AUTHOR, AND BOOGER EXPERT

A GUIDE TO BOOGER COLLECTING

HOW MUCH IS A BOOGER WORTH?

YOU MIGHT BE SURPRISED TO LEARN THAT BOOGERS HAVE SOLD FOR AS MUCH AS TEN MILLION DOLLARS AT AUCTION.

A
BOOGER
PYRAMID

A PREHISTORIC BOOGER ON DISPLAY AT THE MET

THE BOOGER LISA

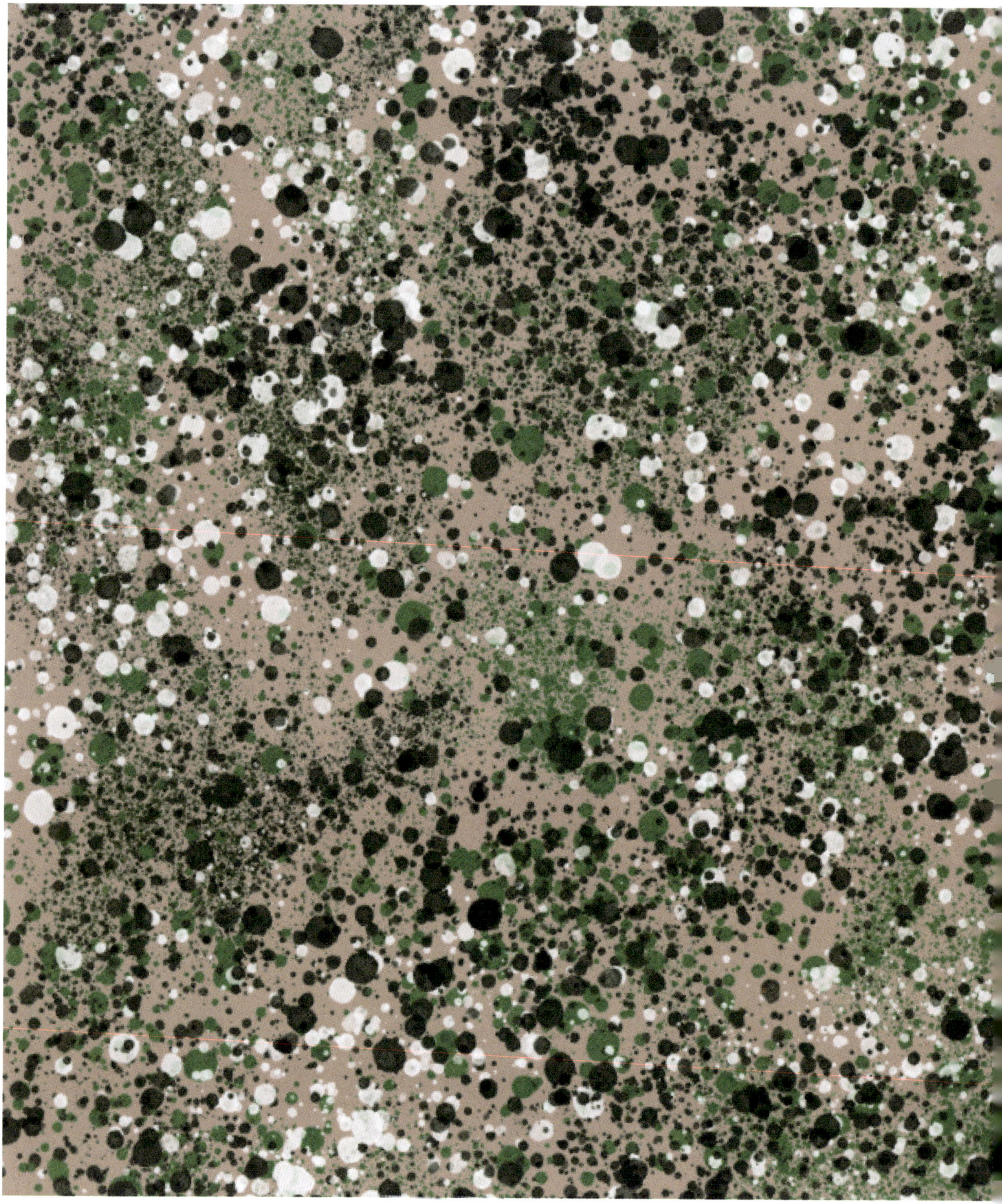

ABSTRACT BOOGER PAINTING, 1951, BOOGER AND PAINT ON CANVAS

WORLD'S LARGEST BOOGER

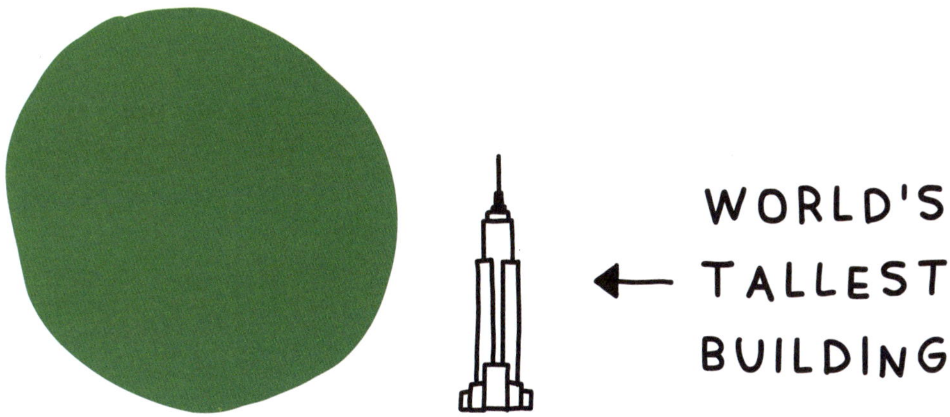
WORLD'S
TALLEST
BUILDING

MR. BOOGER

A RECIPE FOR BOOGER SALAD

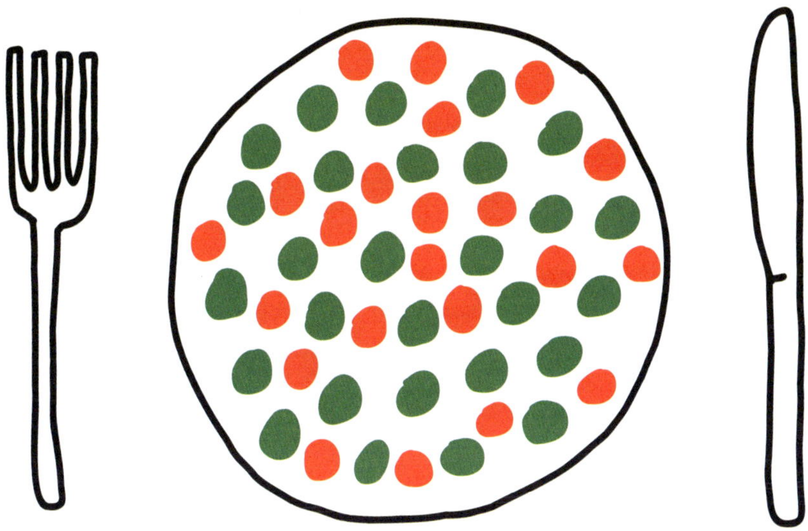

MIXED GREENS
20-30 CHERRY TOMATOES
FRESHLY PICKED BOOGERS

HEY MA! WHAT'S FOR LUNCH?
BOOGER STICKS!
YAY!!!!

BOOGER
EST. 1836
UNIVERSITY

BOOGERS
#1

The Little Booger

THE BOOGER SCREEN

PRIVACY FOR THE
DISCERNING BOOGER PICKER

A SOPHISTICATED BOOGER

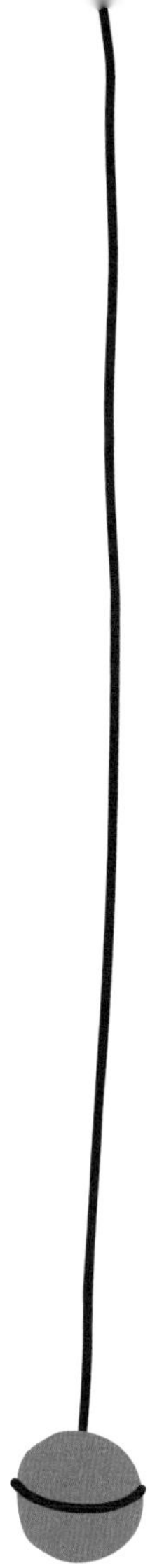

A BUNGEE JUMPING BOOGER

NERD BOOGER

COOL BOOGER

BOO-GER

A BOOGER STRANDED ON A DESERT ISLAND

THE FIRST BOOGER ON THE MOON

WHAT'S FOR DINNER, MA?
BOOGER BURGERS!
YAY!

EVERY BOOGER
HAS A DREAM
BOOGERS!
THE MUSICAL
ON BROADWAY
NOW IN ITS 16TH YEAR!

TEENAGE MUTANT NINJA BOOGERS

LADIES AND GENTLEMEN—
THE BOOGERS!

THE
BOOGERS

AN AMERICAN BOOGER IN PARIS

SUPER

BOOGER!

THE BOOGER KING

BOOGER OR PEA?

PEA OR BOOGER?

HEY MA! WHAT'S FOR DESSERT?
HOMEMADE BOOGER CHIP COOKIES!
YAY !!!!

BOOGER
SODA

Dan's
WORLD FAMOUS
BOOGER
ICE CREAM

BOOGER
ON
BOARD

WELCOME
TO
BOOGERVILLE
POPULATION 19 BOOGERS

LOOKING FORWARD TO SEEING YOU SOON!

GREETINGS
FROM
BOOGER
ISLAND

OTHER BOOKS BY DAN GOLDEN

FAVORITE TOE JAM RECIPES

MORE FAVORITE TOE JAM RECIPES

BELLY LINT—AN INTIMATE HISTORY

EYE BOOGERS, THE "OTHER" BOOGER

EVERYBODY POOPS, AND THAT'S WHY I AVOID EVERYONE

ABOUT DAN GOLDEN

DAN GOLDEN IS AN ARTIST AND DESIGNER WHO LIVES ON BOOGER ISLAND WITH HIS WIFE, JEN, AND THEIR DOG, JUDD. TO LEARN MORE ABOUT DAN, VISIT DANGOLDEN.COM.

THANK YOU

JEN: THANK YOU FOR ALL YOUR HELP AND SUPPORT DEVELOPING THIS BOOK. I LOVE YOU.

ERIN: THANK YOU FOR BEING SUCH A GREAT EDITOR AND BRINGING THIS BOOK INTO THE WORLD. YOU ARE MY "SUPER BOOGER."

I ♥